D. I. Vanderpool
His Stories and Anecdotes

D. I. Vanderpool
His Stories
and
Anecdotes

Compiled by Wilford N. Vanderpool

Edited by Jerald D. Johnson

Nazarene Publishing House
Kansas City, Missouri

ISBN: 083-411-0717

Printed in the
United States of America

10   9   8   7   6   5   4   3   2   1

Contents

Preface

Making satisfactory transitions from stories which have always been presented orally to their written form is more difficult than simply transcribing words and sentences.

Many of the best-known and -loved stories of our father are included in this collection. Each has been faithfully transcribed, some from personal tapes and writings, some from recordings of actual services.

With these transcripts in hand we felt that verbatim publication would make for difficult reading at times. On the other hand, too much editing would destroy the flavor and feeling of our father's original style. We requested our friend and friend of our father, Jerry Johnson, to give us assistance in finalizing these stories for printing.

We feel that the joy and spirit of these personal life stories may be heightened and sharpened by reading them aloud, whether alone or in a family setting.

WILFORD VANDERPOOL

Introduction

In January 1949, Dr. D. I. Vanderpool was elected to serve as a general superintendent in the Church of the Nazarene. His journey of life leading to that momentous occasion was colorful and full of adventure. There were hardships and heartbreaks, but these only helped to forge him into the compassionate and dynamic evangelist he had become.

Dr. Vanderpool was born in 1891 in the state of Missouri. For years he and his brothers lived with their father and grandmother as their parents had separated and then divorced. The eventual remarriage of his parents is a miracle story in itself. This reunion became a strong determining influence in the conversion of Dr. Vanderpool as a young man of 17.

As a lad he was known as Isom or Ike. Some friends called him Vandy or Van. He added the name Daniel himself when he came of age, and ever since then he has been known as D. I.

He joined the Church of the Nazarene in 1912 in Oskaloosa, Iowa. He was attending John Fletcher College, a holiness institution in that town, at the time. Prior to that he had attended McGee Holiness College in College Mound, Mo. Eventually Dr. Vanderpool had opportunity to attend Pasadena College in California and received a degree from that school. Northwest Nazarene College bestowed on him an honorary doctor of divinity degree in 1942.

This man was in the truest sense a pioneer preacher. He knew primitive living before the days of our modern conveniences. He also endured poverty and the accompanying difficulties which would discourage many from feeling they could ever rise from such depths. By God's grace he did just that. Sanctified less than three months after his conversion, he responded to a call to preach. And what a preacher he became!

This compilation of Dr. Vanderpool's stories as he told them, often with tears streaming down his cheeks, will be enjoyed by all who ever heard him preach. He was a master storyteller and communicated great truths of the Bible through the use of personal illustrations.

Even if readers never heard him preach, the stories will be enjoyed. They will provide great reading for family devotions. Young people and children will especially love them.

Preachers who remember Dr. Vanderpool's preaching will feel they have a treasure chest of usable illustrations with this book. And preachers who never heard him will be just as grateful.

At this writing Dr. Vanderpool, at 93 years of age, is still with us. He has outlived two wives and today is cared for in the Village Green Nursing Home in Phoenix. His four children—three sons, who are ordained elders in the Church of the Nazarene, and one daughter—along with grandchildren and now great-grandchildren all consider themselves blessed and fortunate for the marvelous heritage that is theirs.

All of us are recipients of that heritage, and now we have the opportunity of being refreshed with it in the reading of his stories. Here they are, as he told them, compiled by his son Wilford and edited for printing (but done with a sincere endeavor to maintain the typical Vanderpool touch as so many of us affectionately remember hearing them told).

JERALD D. JOHNSON, *Editor**

*The editor was ordained by Dr. D. I. Vanderpool in May 1950. The assignment given him was especially enjoyable because of his deep love and appreciation for the influence of this great man on his own life and ministry.

I

Stories of
God's Redeeming Grace

The Ugly Missourian

Years ago I was conducting a revival campaign in the state of Missouri. Night after night a fellow came in who always sat in the same place, right back of the stove. I thought to myself that he was the ugliest man I had ever seen (and I have seen some pretty hard lookers in my lifetime). In addition it seemed as though this man looked worse night after night. In my mind I thought of him simply as an "ugly Missourian."

One night he seemed to look worse than before. I decided to walk down the aisle and speak to him. I asked, "Brother, are you a Christian?" I was merely trying to make conversation, for I knew he wasn't a child of God. No man could look like he did and be born again. I asked the question anyway: "Are you a Christian?"

He said, "Well, Mr. Vanderpool, I got religion one time, but I guess from what you have been preaching I must have gotten the wrong kind. I never got anything that gave me what you have been talking about."

I said, "Why, Brother, if you didn't get something like that, you sure did get the wrong kind. Come on tonight and get the right kind." His reply was negative, but I persisted, "Come on, get the right kind."

When he said, "No, not tonight," I asked, "Won't you come for one prayer?"

"Well, if you put it that way," he finally responded, "I think I will." He went to the altar and knelt for that one prayer.

After praying with some others at the altar I went over to pray for him. But let me tell you, that fellow had decided if it was just going to be one prayer, and one prayer only, he had better offer that prayer himself. You've never in all your life heard a fellow pray like he did that night.

He prayed and he cried. Rising up on his knees and pushing himself back, he prayed even more earnestly. At one time I thought he was going to fall over backwards.

Finally, he backed up all the way to the front seat and sat there. Then he got down on his knees again and crawled back to the altar. Now he was praying again for all he was worth. When he slowed down a bit I spoke to him. "Brother, how are you getting along?"

He looked up and said, "Mr. Vanderpool, I feel like I'm gettin' the kind of religion you've been talkin' 'bout."

"Praise the Lord," I responded. "Now stay with it, Brother, for you're going to make it if you'll stay with it."

And before you knew it that fellow prayed clear through.

He stood up in the front and began to testify. "I've been a sick man for nearly a year now. I've been to many places trying to get my health back. I left Missouri for Arkansas, hoping I would be better down there." (I'm from Missouri, and frankly I can't understand anyone leaving Missouri for Arkansas.) "But," he went on, "I was no better in Arkansas." (I could understand that.) "Then I went to Oklahoma, on to Kansas, up into Nebraska, and across to Iowa. Nowhere did I feel any better. So I finally came back to Missouri to live out my days in misery. But tonight I got what I have been wanting. I know I found what I've been searching for all across the country."

And you know, God even gave him a face-lift. Along with it he had a new outlook on life. The last I saw him he was indeed a changed man, an ugly Missourian no longer.

The Young Homesteader

In my early days I often preached in remote rural areas. Many of these services were held in tents. It was in one of these meetings that two homesteaders, a young man and an older man, attended with some regularity. The young man got converted. I approached him and urged him to go deeper and dedicate his life fully to the Lord and be sanctified.

He replied, "I really don't know where I would put any more religion than I already have."

I warned him, however, telling him of the dangers of having roots of bitterness still deep within the heart which were not taken care of at the time of conversion.

Two or three nights later I said something while I was preaching which irritated the older homesteader. He jumped up on a chair in the back of the tent, shouting out loud, "That preacher lied tonight." Of course, I was surprised at this outburst but let it pass by. The older man then stomped out of the tent. All of this had obviously upset and angered the younger man, who followed him out of the tent.

When he caught up with the older man, I saw the young man give him a couple of real sharp punches in the ribs with his elbow. "So, the preacher lied, did he?" he shouted. Then he repeated the punches, only harder this time, nearly knocking the old man over. He said it again. "So, the preacher lied, did he?"

The next day when I saw the young man I asked him, "Just how did you feel last night when you nearly broke that man's ribs with those terrible punches you gave him?"

He answered, "I didn't feel very good then, and I don't feel good about it now. I think you're right. I need to get rid of those roots of bitterness you talked to me about."

A night or two later he did dedicate his life and was beautifully sanctified. Later he was even called to preach the gospel.

Seventy Years to Contentment

One doesn't really know anything about real joy until he finds Jesus. I remember seeing a man get converted when he was 70 years of age. Twelve hours after his conversion he was present in a meeting where he stood up and said, "I've been a Christian now for 12 hours, and I want to tell you I've had more enjoyment—real, honest enjoyment—and contentment in these 12 hours than I have known all the former years of my life put together."

He meant just what he said and convinced me of every word of it. He had found real joy, for he had finally met Jesus Christ.

The Hitchhiking Dean

One day I saw a woman standing by the side of the road. She was hitchhiking, endeavoring to thumb a ride into a city about 25 miles away.

About six weeks later I was conducting revival services in a small log church some distance away up in the hills. Much to my surprise, that very same woman whom I had seen hitchhiking came into the church. That night she was gloriously converted. How wonderfully she was saved!

Later on I saw her again. This time I was on the campus of one of our colleges when I met her as the dean of one of the dormitories. Here she exemplified before the students a beautiful Christian life.

As I thought about the tremendous change that had taken place in that woman's life, I stated, "It is simply a marvel what the grace of God can do for people."

He Agreed to Serve God in Hell

In a certain community where I was preaching, a man informed me he had been saved years ago but was not a Christian at the time. "For 35 years I have known I am a lost man and that there is no hope for me." He said he had gone too far away from God to get back to Him.

I said to him, "But you don't need to be lost, for Jesus said, 'Come unto me, *all* ye that labour,' and that includes you."

When I persisted he replied, "No, I can't do it. I have sought Him and sought Him, but He won't answer. He doesn't even hear me."

I asked, "But have you really and earnestly been willing to give up your sins?"

He said he was, but still insisted, "God won't hear me."

I then said, "The next time you pray, tell God that even if He sends you to hell, you are going to serve Him there." His eyes opened big, for he was startled at the idea of anyone serving God in hell. I continued, "You could just sort of start a kind of revolution there. Go ahead, make up your mind you're going to serve God in this life, and then if He sends you to hell, you'll serve Him there."

A few nights later the old boy came into a service where I was preaching and piled into the altar. He was wonderfully and gloriously saved that very night. It's true. If a man makes up his mind that he is going out of the sin business, that he is really through with it once and for all, he can be saved.

A Broken Home Reunited

One night during the course of a revival meeting I was conducting, a lady and her little girl came into the service. When I finished preaching the lady came to the altar and was gloriously converted. She wept a great deal, and one could sense she carried a heavy burden.

After the service I inquired about her. I was told who she was and that her husband had left her about three months before. The little girl was especially brokenhearted because her daddy had left. I commented that the mother had certainly received victory that evening and appeared happy in finding salvation.

I then asked where her husband could be found. I was informed he was shucking corn about 20 miles away. When I further asked about the possibility of getting him into church, the reply was negative.

However, three or four nights later I saw this rather hard-looking old codger come into the service. Sure enough, it was the husband and father about whom I had inquired. I preached the best I knew how, and when I gave the invitation to come to the altar he stood right up, walked to the front, and knelt down. On the other side of the church were his wife and little girl. Immediately his wife came up and knelt beside him, putting an arm about him. They both prayed. Tears were shed, and it wasn't long until that ol' boy prayed through. They stood to their feet, facing the crowd, giving testimony to finding salvation.

The next night they were back in church, all three of them together. After the service he spoke to me and said, "Brother Vanderpool, I'd like for you to come over to our house and set up a family altar. I don't know how to do it myself, and if you'd come over and do it for me I sure would appreciate it."

I told him, "I'll be over."

In their home I read the Bible to them and then asked all of them to get on their knees with me and I would pray for them. In my prayer I asked God to open heaven on that home.

Years later, 25 to be exact, I was preaching in Hutchinson, Kans. Down the aisle with his wife by his side walked this same gentleman. With the two of them was their daughter, now a young mother herself with her own little child in her arms.

"Do you remember me, Brother Vanderpool?" he asked.

Twenty-five years had made a lot of difference and I had to admit, "Sir, I don't believe I do."

He continued, "Do you remember a fellow who asked you to come into his home and set up a family altar for him?"

That event I could remember, and I asked, "Are you that fellow?"

He replied, "I am, Brother Vanderpool, and I want you to know the fire has never burned out in all these 25 years."

It's true, you know. When God comes into the heart it makes a tremendous change. Jesus said, "Come unto me, all ye that labour and are heavy laden, and I will give you rest" (Matt. 11:28). Thank God for this message given to sinners everywhere.

The Forty-two-year Burden

Years ago when I was serving as a pastor I greeted a man who had come to the parsonage door. He was a gentleman in his late 60s who appeared to be in great distress. I invited him into the living room where he sat down on the couch and began to share his burden. "I've got such a problem," he declared, "that I don't know what to do." He went on by saying he had carried this burden for 42 years and felt he needed help in dealing with it.

As I listened I finally suggested, "Well, tell me about it."

He then told me his story. "I was born in the old country. Forty-two years ago I had trouble and decided to leave. I came to America and changed my name. I married under this assumed name and raised my family with it. For 42 years I have had this guilt, and I don't know what to do about it."

As we talked I sensed he was terribly distressed over the matter. Frankly I couldn't see that changing his name should be such a problem; a lot of women do that, you know, when they marry. It seemed to me that when he came to America he had left much of that behind him. After all, he had left England 42 years before, and I didn't see how he could return and straighten matters out. I felt the best thing for him was to let the curtain drop and trust the mercy of God. I said to him, "I believe you should confess to Christ and tell Him you're sorry, sorry, sorry you ever got messed up; then just trust God to forgive you."

There at the couch he knelt. We didn't pray together longer than five minutes when he joyfully exclaimed, "It is done. He forgives me." His long and heavy burden was obviously lifted from him.

We stood and shook hands with one another. I then urged him, "Now that you've told it all to God, just forget the whole business. Forget what your old name was and just hang on to the name you've got now. Leave it in God's hands. He blots out the past and fixes everything up."

He became a happy man. Later he joined the church. It was simply marvelous what happened to him when he really came to Christ and asked for forgiveness. It's a wonderful thing how most of our problems can be solved when we turn them over to God.

No Promise of Tomorrow

Years ago as I preached, I observed a young lady in the back of the church. Her name was Nina, a 19-year-old who had begun attending our church. It was something I rarely did, but that night, feeling so burdened and concerned about Nina, I slipped back during the altar call and spoke personally with her, asking her if she would go to the altar.

She looked at me and said, "No, Brother Vanderpool, I've made up my mind. I'm not going to start anymore until I know I can live the Christian life."

I asked her, "But, Nina, how do you know you are going to have a long time to try to live it?"

This seemed to cause her to think seriously about the matter. She finally replied, "Well, if you put it that way, maybe I'd better go tonight." She then went to the altar.

She was wonderfully and blessedly saved that Sunday evening. On the following Wednesday evening she was present in prayer meeting. She testified as to how wonderful Monday, Tuesday, and that Wednesday had been. She then went to the altar again, dedicating her life to God, who sanctified her.

The next day, Thursday afternoon, she was involved in a serious accident at the place where she worked. I was informed that if I ever expected to see Nina alive again I would have to hurry to the hospital. Walking into her room, I saw that life was indeed ebbing away. She was conscious, however, and as I walked through the door, I thought maybe her eyes sparkled a little. She was glad to see me. I walked over, placed my hand on hers, and asked, "Nina, how is everything?"

"Oh," she replied. "Everything is all right. I'm glad I went forward last Sunday night and got everything all fixed up." Within two hours Nina slipped away to be with her Lord.

The Drug Addict

Years ago in a service where I was preaching a little lady came to the altar to pray at the conclusion of a Sunday morning service. During the time of prayer I went to her and asked, "Lady, what is it you are seeking?"

With tears in her eyes she looked up at me and admitted, "Rev. Vanderpool, I'm a drug addict. I'm bound by drugs and need help. Just last evening I had to send my two little girls away from home for fear I might kill them. I need God to set me free."

Another minister was close by, and I asked him to join me at the altar. We both knelt and laid hands on this lady, at the same time asking God to break the shackles that bound her, giving her deliverance and setting her free from drug addiction. In less than five minutes she looked up with a new light in her eyes, declaring, "I believe He does it."

Five years later I saw that lady again. She told me that from that morning on she hadn't had one problem with drug addiction.

We have a Savior who saves to the uttermost. This includes all who come to Him in genuine sincerity and repentance. He will save them.

II

Stories of
God's Providing Care

The Little Westside Bank

During the Great Depression of the 30s I served as pastor of First Church of the Nazarene in Denver. It was a difficult time. Many people were unemployed. Stores were going bankrupt, and many of the banks were closing for the same reason.

Not far from our church was the location of a small bank known as the Westside Bank. As I read that banks in nearby cities such as Longmont, Loveland, and Canon City were closing, I wondered to myself how long it would be until the little Westside Bank would have to close its doors as well.

One day just a few weeks later, I noted a long line of people standing before the doors of this little bank. In my mind I said, Good-bye, little bank. However, I observed the bank remained open all day, and closed at its usual closing time.

The next morning another line formed in front of the bank. At its regular opening time the doors opened and the people took their turns drawing out all the money they had in their personal savings accounts.

About eleven o'clock when one of the men arrived at the cashier's window asking if he could have his money, he was startled to see the teller begin to count it out. Suddenly the man was heard to say, "Why, if I can get my money, then I really don't want it."

The customer behind him asked the teller if he would be able to get his money. The teller assured him also that he could. His reply was similar. "Then I don't want mine either."

Just as quickly as it started, the run on the little bank was over. The line began to break up and the people departed.

If I had known the whole story I would not have worried about the little bank. The facts were that the Westside Bank was but a branch of the First National Bank of Denver. This meant that all the assets of the big bank downtown were there to offset any liabilities the little bank out our way might have. While customers were withdrawing their deposits out the front door, armored trucks were delivering bales of money in the back door.

As I thought about that little bank I began to think about my assets with God. He has untold resources of strength and joy and peace, just to name a few. All we need to do is "ask" that we might receive, "seek" that we might find, and "knock" that it all shall be opened to us (Matt. 7:7-8). His assets are unlimited. We need not fear they shall be drained.

Bible School Days

I was preparing to attend a Bible school which was located in College Mound, Mo. I was, however, very short of money, and when I went to get my train ticket I had only a few cents in my pocket. As I went up to the ticket window to make the purchase I found I was 25 cents short. I stepped back, and there was a man I knew, J. F. Watkins, whom I had met at a camp meeting a few weeks before. In fact, he had talked me into going to Bible school. He asked if I had my ticket. When I told him I didn't he wanted to know why. I explained that I lacked 25 cents of having enough money. In a flash his hand came out of his pocket with a quarter in it, and he said, "Now, go get your ticket." Brother Watkins purchased a ticket for himself as he intended to travel with me to the school.

We got off the train at Excello, about five miles from College Mound. I knew I could walk the distance, but my friend paid another 10 cents for me to ride in a wagon with him. We arrived in the little village which consisted of a store, a wood frame post office building, a small bank, a few residences, and an orphanage. Of course, there was also the Bible school, McGee Holiness College, with its two frame dormitory buildings of about eight rooms each, a printing press and office, and the brick administration building with classrooms, a library, and a chapel. There were no dining facilities. Most of the students would get their room and board in homes in the community.

As I got down from the wagon an elderly preacher stepped up to me and asked if I was coming to school. When I told him I was he asked me to come to his house for the noon meal. I gladly accepted the invitation, and before dinner was over I had agreed to work for him; in return I would get room and board, and his family would do my laundry for me. My job was to care for two cows night and morning, carry coal and wood upstairs for two rooms, and help clean house on Saturdays.

After we had agreed to these arrangements I went over to the school to see about registering for classes. Professor Batchler was both president and business manager. After greeting me he asked about my ability to pay cash for my tuition. I told him of my financial plight and then asked if I could perhaps work it out.

The professor told me they needed someone to sweep and dust two classrooms five days each week and carry out trash cans Wednesdays and Fridays. In return I would get my tuition. I said I would do these jobs as long as the man giving me room and board agreed. He did so, and this meant that all my needs would be met.

As word got around that I had been able to get everything settled by five o'clock on the day I had arrived without even a penny in my pocket, there seemed to be general consensus that God had been directing in my coming to College Mound. I'll admit that there were a few times I wondered why they thought I had such a wonderful deal.

In addition to the above assignments I had one more in connection with my tuition. On Thursdays I was to turn the washing machine for two hours at noontime. It just so happened that Thursday noons were set aside for fasting at that school.

I must say now, however, that I learned some lessons then that have literally been a godsend to me across the years.

Prayer for a Postage Stamp

While I was attending McGee Holiness College in College Mound, Mo., a young man came and enrolled who stayed only about three months. During this time he was converted. After he had been gone about a month he wrote me, asking that I send him a letter of encouragement. He referred to deep spiritual struggles in his life.

My problem was that I didn't have a stamp or the money to buy one. Yet I thought if I didn't write and he got discouraged and backslid, I'd always feel I let him down. So I thought I would write the letter and trust God for the stamp.

After writing the letter I went down to the little post office, knowing the postman would soon be arriving in town. The post office was next to the bank. I watched the postman as he drove in and began sorting the mail. As I stood there, I heard tapping on the inside of the bank window. Turning around, I saw one of the Bible school teachers, Dr. A. E. Sanner. He motioned for me to come in. As I stepped inside he shook my hand, leaving a silver dollar in it.

I took it without a word of thanks. I knew if I tried to say anything I would cry or shout or create a scene. I stepped over to the post office, bought a stamp, and mailed my letter. I then went immediately to a little clump of trees away from the town and school campus where I had gone many times to be alone and pray. There I thanked God for His answer to my prayer and went on my way rejoicing.

My New Coat

One day while still in Bible school I looked at my only coat. It was old, faded, and showed signs of hard use. I prayed about it, telling the Lord I needed a new coat. As I prayed, "Please, Lord, give me a new coat," I seemed to get an answer right away, assuring me that He would give me a new coat. I was happy and felt blessed about it.

We had been taught in Bible school that when we prayed through about something, we should witness to the fact to at least two or three people. So I shared with two of my friends that I had prayed through for a new coat.

One day went by and there was no new coat. Two days, still no coat. Three days, and there was no new coat. It seemed, however, that each time I prayed He would let me know he would give me a new coat. The word had gotten around, and it seemed as though everybody was looking to see me wear my new coat.

One day I went up to the school's bell tower. I wanted to get as close to heaven as possible. I prayed, "Dear Lord, You promised me a new coat, and I have told others about it. Please, Lord, I want my coat today."

Like a flash He seemed to answer back, "I will give you your coat today." I laughed and shouted.

As I came down from the tower, I heard someone pounding on the front door of the chapel. I opened the door, and there stood Isaiah Buchanan. He said, "I have been wanting to see you." He told me that he had seen Brother T. A. Mercer a couple of days before, and he was looking for me. "Maybe you should go see him," he suggested.

I thought to myself, My coat!

I walked out to Brother Mercer's house, about a quarter of a mile from town, and knocked on his door. As he opened it he said, "Why, Brother Vanderpool, I have been wanting to see you for the past several days."

Then he told of being at a little country church where he was serving as pastor. A lady in the church who was the mother of three boys had purchased a new suit for each of her boys. When pressing the pants for one of the suits she let the iron get too hot and burned a hole in them. She had to buy another suit.

Because she now had a coat left over, she spoke to Brother Mercer, asking if there might be a young man up at the Bible school who could use a new coat. Brother Mercer said, "I brought the coat along, and if it fits then you may have it."

I replied immediately, "Get the coat; it will fit."

It did fit perfectly, and I wore that coat for several years. Many times I have thought that if everybody had only cooperated with God a little better, I would have had my coat in less time! But I was glad for the answer and praised God for it.

God Promised Me a Soul

Years ago when I was a young evangelist, having been preaching for only about three years, I was requested to help another evangelist in a revival meeting he was conducting in a country church. When I arrived I found the evangelist to be quite ill with tuberculosis. He couldn't visit the people or do anything other than preach. We both stayed at the same place. I was younger than he. I suppose he was 35 to 40 years of age.

The lady of the house was partial to him. Because he had tuberculosis she gave him special attention, feeding him not only very well, but always punctually as well as adequately. Now I didn't have tuberculosis, so I was fed another fare — not always adequate and not always on time.

This man was a good preacher. Our schedule called for each of us to preach every other night. The meeting began, and after each had preached two nights neither of us had experienced seekers coming to the altar.

Two of the men of the church came to me and said, "Brother Vanderpool, it seems to us that the spirit to preach is on this other evangelist, and we believe the spirit to pray is on you. We think it would be better if you don't preach anymore and just let him do all the preaching. You pray and let him preach."

"Well," I replied, "all right, if that's the way you feel about it I'll sure do my best to pray."

But then they went on, "It is your turn to preach tomorrow night, so you go ahead and preach tomorrow night and let the other brother take over from then on."

The next morning I went to the woods to pray. I knelt down on a flat-topped rock under a big oak tree and began to pray. It was about 9:30 in the morning. Squirrels came by and barked at me. Birds flew around chirping and chattering at me. I prayed on.

About 3:30 in the afternoon the Lord came very near to me. He blessed me and said, "I'll give you a soul tonight." I got happy just knowing God would give me a soul that night.

I remembered what we had learned at school. If you prayed through on a matter it should be shared as a witness to at least two or three people so that "in the mouth of two or three witnesses every word may be established" (Matt. 18:16). At about 4 P.M. when I got back to the house where I was staying I was prepared to share my assurance with our hostess and the other evangelist.

Upon my arrival she said, "Well, you've certainly been out all day."

I said, "Yes, and I've had a good time praying. The Lord has promised me a soul tonight."

I then turned to the preacher and declared, "The Lord has promised me a soul tonight." I was doing my witnessing as I had been taught to do. The preacher stared back at me as though I had been premature in my announcement.

At six o'clock it began to cloud up. Then it thundered as lightning began to flash. It was a bad storm which had come up suddenly and without warning. Then it began to rain. In fact, it poured.

I knew the water would soon be up to the little footlog we used for crossing over into the church, and if I didn't leave soon I might not be able to get into the church building. As soon as I finished eating I said, "Well, I think I'll go on over to the church."

The two of them said, "Oh no, there's no use in going. There won't be anyone there tonight. This storm will keep them all away."

"Well," I said, "I am going anyway." The other evangelist thought that just in case someone did show up, it would look bad if I went and he didn't. So he decided to tag along. He grumbled all the way, saying something about running fool's errands and being on a wild goose chase. He knew no one would be there. I felt sorry for him, for he did have tuberculosis and we got all wet and cold. I certainly didn't ask him to come, but he was with me nevertheless.

When we arrived the church was empty. We went in, sat down, and waited. About 7:30 he said, "Let's go home. Nobody's coming."

I said, "No, I'm going to wait."

Fifteen minutes later he said again, "Let's go home. We're just sitting here getting chilled, and no one's coming."

Now don't think for a moment that I was having an easy time of it. I was, in fact, having the worst time of my life. The devil spoke to me and said, "You should have kept your big mouth shut and not told them about praying through. You just should have kept quiet."

In my mind I was trying to reassure myself that I did what I thought was right. Then I prayed, "It's just up to You, Lord. I don't know how I am going to get out of this. God, You will just have to help me."

It was eight o'clock when we heard footsteps at the door of the church. Stomp, stomp, stomp. Then a man I recognized as a near neighbor of the church came in. In fact, I had talked to him when I had been out visiting and had asked him to come to church. He had said, "Well, I never liked to go to church. When they get around that altar with different ones praying at the same time, there's so much confusion that I can't even hear myself think. I just don't like it."

But there he was, the same man. He was wearing a raincoat and hat as well as big rubber boots. After he had shaken the rain off himself and come in, I said, "All right, Brother Garrett, come on down. We've been waiting for you."

He took off his raincoat and hat, laid them on a bench, and walked straight to the altar. There weren't a lot of people to pray and confuse him that night. He could simply have one quiet time in which to get through to God. Earnestly he prayed, and in a little while he rose up wonderfully saved. God had verified His promise to me. And then I got happy. You know, I was a little demonstrative in those days, and I began to shout. The piano was a flat-topped, three-legged affair, and when I quit shouting I found myself up on top of that piano.

When we got home our hostess met us at the door. "Well, Brother Vanderpool," she said rather sarcastically, "did you get that soul you said you were going to get tonight?"

I replied that we had.

She looked surprised. "You did? Who was it?"

I told her, "It was that brother of yours for whom you and your mother have prayed for over 20 years."

She said, "You mean that Hal got saved tonight?"

I assured her, "Yes, he was gloriously converted."

She came over and took me by the hand. "Forgive me, Brother Vanderpool. Please forgive me. I'm so sorry."

But there's a further great climax to this story. For the rest of the revival meeting she fed me as though I had tuberculosis too.

A Pioneer Healer

An elderly Swedish mother shared an incident with me that took place when her children were small. Her oldest son, seven years old, had come down with typhoid fever. He was very ill, and it appeared he could not live through the day.

The mother was a born-again Christian and turned to the Bible for comfort. She read James 5:14-15: "Is any sick among you? let him call for the elders of the church; and let them pray over him, anointing him with oil in the name of the Lord: and the prayer of faith shall save the sick, and the Lord shall raise him up."

She knew it was too far into town to get the doctor. Besides, she reminded herself that Emil needed help right then. And where could she get an elder?

Then she began to reason to herself. "I am no youngster myself. I am 34 years old. That makes me an elder. I have no oil, but I do have some meat fryings in the skillet."

First she washed her hands. Then she took some grease from the skillet and went over to where Emil was lying unconscious on his bed. She prayed a little prayer saying, "I am 34 years old. I have no oil, just this grease. Now, Lord, when I put this on little Emil's head, please touch him." As she wiped the grease on his forehead, she said, "Amen."

In about 10 seconds the little boy opened his eyes, stretched a bit, and, seeing his mother, said, "Ma, I'm hungry." She asked, "What do you want?" He said, "I want some beans."

She dipped a bowl of beans for him from a pot on the back of the stove. He ate them, and in a few days he was as well as ever.

I saw Emil myself when he was 25 years old. He could hardly remember when he had been sick. The good health he was enjoying was the result of the prayer and faith of his pioneer mother.

Determination Pays Off

Many years ago when I was conducting a revival meeting in La Junta, Colo., an elderly woman approached me. She greeted me with, "Brother Vanderpool, my husband is not a Christian. But I have had the feeling that if he is ever won to Christ it will have to be in this revival meeting. Furthermore, you are the one to win him."

"No, no," I said, "you can't put that on me."

"But that's the way I feel," she continued. "If he is ever won, you'll have to win him."

I asked if he came to church. She responded, "He hasn't been to church in 35 years. He's a hard man, and he hates preachers. But I still feel you are the one to win him."

That was quite an assignment. I thought a bit about this woman's sincerity and finally asked, "If he doesn't come to church, how do you expect me to win him? I'll need your help. I want you to invite me to your place for dinner."

She invited me to come the next day.

When I went there the husband met me at the door. I noticed his eyes seemed to bother him, and I felt he couldn't see very well. I greeted him with, "Good morning. I'm holding a revival meeting over in a tent set up by the post office, and your wife invited me to have dinner with you."

His only reply was, "Uh huh."

I continued, "So I came over."

Again he said, "Uh huh."

His wife came out of the kitchen about that time, saw me at the door, got past her husband, and let me in. He just glanced at me while she tried to make introductions. "Brother Vanderpool, this is my husband. Sit down in that chair over there."

She pointed to a rocking chair, and I said, "No, no. Here, Dad, you sit in the rocker, and I'll take a straight-backed one here." He continued to glare and I thought, He's resenting my bossing him around.

As he sat he put his hands over his face and wouldn't talk. I tried to make conversation. "Dad, do your eyes hurt you?"

Finally he spoke. "If you had ridden the prairies as I have and been where I have been, your eyes would hurt you, too."

"Oh, have you been on the prairies in sandstorms, perhaps?"

"Yes. I've been around these parts a long time and had lots of experiences. My father and Kit Carson were good friends." He told of a cold winter day out on the mountain

36

when his horse slipped and he fell off, breaking a leg. "I knew I would freeze to death," he said. "But I hadn't been lying there more than five minutes when I heard hoofbeats. A man leading a packhorse came and picked me up, taking me to a doctor. He saved my life. I never even got frostbite."

At the table his wife asked me to pray. I was soft and gentle in my praying, not wanting to offend the old fellow. Later I said, "Dad, come and hear me preach."

He just laughed and said, "The tent will fall down if I come in under it."

Quickly I said, "Let's risk it. I'll tighten up the stakes and you can come on in." I grinned at him. "Just come and hear me preach one time. You haven't been to church in a long time, and it's not a church anyway. It's a tent."

Finally he said, "All right, I'll come just once."

He did not come that night nor the next. When I commented on this to his wife she said, "Yes, I know, and he sure wishes he hadn't promised."

I said, "It looks like you're going to have to invite me to dinner again."

When I went back to their home he met me at the door again. But things were different. He grabbed me by the hand and ushered me in himself.

I said to him, "You know, Dad, I've been thinking about you. God has certainly been good to you. You told me how you could have frozen to death, but a man with a packhorse came along and saved your life. You didn't even get frostbite. Now can't you see how good God has been to you and spared you? You have a wife and family with three of your boys, along with your wife, on their way to heaven. And you, you're not on your way to that better land."

It was time to eat. This time when I prayed it was not soft and gentle as before. I began to pray for all I was worth. I prayed for him. I prayed for his boys. I prayed that the entire family would be united someday in a better world. And God helped me to pray.

When we finally finished eating we pulled our chairs back and I said, "Dad, I'd like to see you give your heart to Jesus and really be a genuine Christian."

He looked at me and said, "Well, I'm ready." He dropped to his knees right where he had been sitting, and the old boy prayed through. He was wonderfully and gloriously converted.

A month later I came back through La Junta, and someone asked if I had heard about old Brother Nelson. "He had a stroke," I was told, so I went to see him.

His left side was paralyzed and he had lost his voice. He motioned to me, and his wife said, "I think he wants you to pray." I knelt by his bed, and he raised his good hand in praise to God while I prayed.

There was a picture hanging on the wall depicting Jesus with a lamb in His arms. He motioned for his wife to take the picture down and bring it to him. He took the picture and held it close to his chest. I got the message. He was the lamb, and he was safe in the arms of Jesus. A week later he passed away.

What I am trying to say is that if some people are going to be saved we will have to show some determination. We can't quit too soon. It may take time and prayer and love. And it also takes action to make a difference in the lives of the unsaved. But in the end it pays great dividends.

Praying in the Spirit

Years ago I was in Nampa, Idaho, as one of two preachers for a camp meeting. The other evangelist was a lady, Stella Crooks. We had three services a day and took turns about on the preaching schedule.

On Saturday evening a group of 25 to 30 men remained after the service for a prayer meeting. We were praying that the next day would be a great closing day of the camp. As we were praying we observed that the song evangelist, Harold Hart, came to join us. He was a big man who came to where we were and dropped to his knees as he began to pray. You have never heard a fellow pray as he did. He laid hold of the bell rope of heaven and began to pull. Finally as he climaxed his prayer he pled, "O God, give us 100 souls tomorrow."

That was a big prayer. He did seem to be praying in the Spirit. I'll admit to thinking while he prayed for 100 souls that there weren't that many fish in the pond. But that's the way he prayed, anyway.

It was my turn to preach on Sunday morning. I preached the best I could and opened the altar. Seventeen people came forward for prayer.

Stella Crooks preached a tremendous message in the afternoon service. She too opened the altar and another 18 came forward. I got out my pencil and added the two figures together, noting that a total of 35 had been to the altar. I said to myself, "If that prayer is to be answered we've got to have 65 at the altar tonight." I prayed for the evening service and asked God to help us.

That night I preached the best I could. The tent was full. In addition, cars were parked all around which were also full of people. How the Lord did help me preach. I was just beginning to give the altar call when a little lady near the front jumped to her feet and began to shout. She jumped up and down, making a lot of noise, even screaming. It was unimaginable that one little woman could make so much noise. Here I was trying to give an invitation, and this woman was breaking my "net" all to pieces.

I was satisfied this woman was out of order, so I just stepped over the altar to where she was bouncing around and said, "Mother, sit down and be quiet." But she didn't and she wouldn't. Finally I put my hand on her head with, I suppose, about 40 pounds of pressure. That settled her down and I said, "Now, Mother, sit down and be quiet." I then proceeded with the altar call.

Suddenly I heard the doors of cars slamming all around the tent in the park. People began to come into the tent, down the aisles, and to the altar. Soon they were kneeling at the front bench as the altar was filled. The district superintendent, Dr. Sanner, leaned over to me and said, "Brother Vanderpool, I just counted 66 at the altar."

After the service was over I went to the little lady who had made so much commotion and said, "Mother, forgive me. I didn't mean to be rude to you."

She looked at me and asked, "What made me do that? I believe the devil made me do what I did."

I said, "No, I wouldn't say that. I wouldn't say that at all."

As I look back upon it I'm inclined to believe maybe that little woman was in divine order. But I also think I was in divine order. When she shouted and carried on as she did, those people in their parked cars had to get out and come over to the tent to see what was going on. That brought them into the atmosphere of the service, and there God smote them.

Now, after all these years I have thought about how Harold Hart prayed in the Spirit.

We all need to learn to pray in the Spirit in order to see what God is really able to do.

Veiled Providence

One Sunday morning when I was a district superintendent I was in one of the churches on my district for a service. A lady came up to me and said, "Brother Vanderpool, please pray for me. I'm going through a terrible trial. I have a

17-year-old boy who is with my unsaved husband out fishing today. If they weren't fishing they would be golfing. I go to church alone while it looks as though my husband is taking my boy further from God and the church in spite of my own efforts otherwise. It looks as though I am going to lose my boy." She cried as she talked.

I said, "Lady, you'll just have to trust God to help you. Leave the boy in God's hands and pray for God to undertake."

A year later I was back in that same church. This same lady came to me and said, "Brother Vanderpool, the worst has come. My boy was drafted into the army, and he's stationed out on the East Coast." She went on, "Now he'll be among those wicked soldiers and live like they do. I'm afraid I'll lose him. He never will get straightened out."

Four months later I was once again in the same church. This time I was greeted at the door by a nice-looking gentleman who shook hands with me. As I spoke to him the same little mother came over and spoke to me. Her face was all covered with smiles. "Brother Vanderpool," she said, "this is my husband. He has been converted. He's a Christian now. We are so happy. He joined the church last Sunday. Everything is just fine now."

I looked at her and said, "There must be a story behind all this."

She said, "Yes," and proceeded to relate it to me.

When her boy was sent to the East Coast he became very homesick and lonesome. He began to think about his mother's church. He sought out the Church of the Nazarene and attended several services. The people were nice and friendly to him, taking him into their homes for meals and letting him know they were interested in him. Soon he was converted.

He then wrote his father a letter. "Dad," he wrote, "I've been converted and I need your help. While I was still running around at home I picked up and stole different things. Now I've got to make restitution for them. But I can't do it myself." He reckoned he owed about $42.00 in different places. He explained the items and the places and, along with a check for the entire amount, asked his father if he would make the restitution for him. "It will be a wonderful relief to me," he concluded.

The dad loved his boy. They had hunted, fished, and played golf together. Although not a Christian himself, the letter got to him; and because of his interest in the boy, he took the money and starting making the rounds to clear things up. By the time he had gone to several places the father decided he had to make some restitution himself, get converted, and begin to serve God. The result was the salvation of the entire family.

Now what that lady interpreted to be the worst that could happen turned out to be a veiled providence. God was using the circumstances to save both her husband and her son. There is a lesson in this for all of us. If things seem to go wrong for a while, don't get discouraged, don't give up. Just hang on and claim the promises. Expect God to work things out for His glory and bring you through triumphantly. Just as sure as you hold steady and are true to God, He will not fail you.

III

Stories of
God's Guiding Hand

The Old Dutchman

An evangelist friend of mine was conducting a camp meeting. He was enjoying himself during the camp when one day an old Dutchman came and spoke to him. "I'd like for you to come and hold a camp meeting for me," he said.

My startled evangelist friend replied, "Well, sir, I'd be glad to do so, but do you have a church?"

"Oh, no, I don't have a church."

"Well then, are you a preacher?"

"No, I'm not a preacher. I just want you to come and hold a camp meeting for me."

My friend said, "Well, I don't have any open dates just now, but if I should have an opening I will give it consideration." The Dutchman was satisfied and that ended the conversation.

Within a short time my friend did have a cancellation, and he thought about the Dutchman. He sent word to him saying, "I can come and give you 10 days right away, which means there is little or no time to advertise."

The answer was immediate. Instructions were given to come on over. He was told the little town where he should get off the train. The arrangements were completed.

When my evangelist friend arrived at the little town it turned out to be little indeed. In fact, it was what we called a jerkwater town. When he got off he looked for the Dutchman. He was nowhere to be found. My friend thought, I sure drew a lemon this time.

After a bit a man came up and said to him, "Are you the evangelist who has come to hold a meeting?" My friend replied that he was.

The stranger said, "Come on, get in my rig here, and I'll take you out to where the camp meeting is to be held."

My friend exclaimed, "On out! How can it be on out? Isn't this far enough out already?"

Riding along, my friend asked the stranger, "Do you know this old Dutchman?"

"Yes. Do you know him?"

"No, I really don't. What kind of fellow is he?"

The driver said, "Well, he is kind of a queer ol' duck."

"Why do you say that?"

"Just wait and you'll see."

They rounded the top of a hill and saw a board fence three-quarters of a mile long. Scripture verses had been printed all over the fence with words like, "Blessed are the pure in heart: for they shall see God" (Matt. 5:8); "The blood of Jesus Christ his Son cleanseth us from all sin" (1 John 1:7); "Without . . . holiness . . . no man shall see the Lord" (Heb. 12:14).

The driver said, "You see that on the fence? That old man paid hard money to have that painted. That should tell you one reason why I say he is a queer ol' duck."

They drove on to another hill. From there they could see the old Dutchman's barn. All along the wide roof was written "Holiness unto the Lord." It could be seen from a long distance away. The driver said, "Now you really know a man is different when he does something like that!"

The evangelist asked, "But is he a good neighbor? Is he honest?"

"Oh yes, he's a good neighbor and an honest man."

When they arrived they were greeted by the old Dutchman. "I'm glad you came," he said. "I'm sorry I couldn't meet

46

you at the depot, but we have been preparing for the meeting. We are trusting the Lord to give us a good one."

My friend commented about the shortness of time as far as advertising was concerned.

The Dutchman replied, "But the people will be here. I've been telling them all about it."

"But you haven't had much time to tell them you are going to have a camp meeting. When did you first tell them?"

"Oh, about eight years ago I told them I was going to have a camp meeting. I've been telling them ever since, and I believe they will be here."

That night the services started. People came in horse-drawn buggies and old cars. A brush arbor had been put up, and the people seemed to file in from everywhere.

When the evangelist rose to preach he sensed the power of the Spirit moving on the place. He normally never gave an altar call the first night of a meeting, but that night he did. The people knelt all along the altar and at the edge of the platform. Thirty came forward the very first night. As the evangelist worked his way among the seekers he would ask what their prayer need was. Over and over came the reply, "I want what the old Dutchman has. I want what the old Dutchman has."

For 20 years a Spirit-filled, sanctified man had lived in that community. Now God was using his life and influence to reach the lives of many.

Dad's Hand on the Wheel

I was riding in the backseat of a car. The driver and his wife were in the front. Between them was their little boy in a little chair arrangement. He was secured in the seat so he could not fall out. Attached was a little wheel much like his daddy's steering wheel. The little lad could hold it, turn it, and steer with it as though he were driving the car. From where I sat I could see his every move.

He did have a good grip on the little steering wheel. He turned it to the right and then to the left. He turned it fast, then slow. And always he was laughing, yelling, and having the time of his life. He thought he was driving the car. Of course, I knew better.

From where I sat I couldn't see the pair of big hands which really steered the car. But I knew they were on the wheel. What a difference between little hands on a little wheel that was not a part of the car and big hands on the wheel that controls the car.

How much we are like the little boy. Many times we laugh, shout, or weep because of some turn life may take. But there is One greater than we are who is in control. If only we could grasp what Paul said, "We know that all things work together for good to them that love God, to them who are the called according to his purpose" (Rom. 8:28).

Called to Preach

Once in a while when I was district superintendent I made a hit. Other times I missed it, but occasionally I made it. One day a fellow approached me and said, "I want to be a preacher."

Well, he didn't look like he would make much of a preacher. He wasn't trained and the years were already catching up with him. He had a good job and a nice home. Now he was planning to sell his house. He was persistent. "I want a church. Don't you have one for me?"

"Well," I said, "I do have a church. The salary is $15.00 a week. There is an old two-room parsonage, and the walls and furniture in it are already inhabited."

I painted as dark a picture as I could. When I finished describing the parsonage I began talking about the church building. It was a rented building. The stovepipes were held up with baling wire. At that, the pipes didn't fit well together. The front door was barely hanging. You had to get hold of the knob and lift or heave to get the door shut or open. I thought after I pictured it to him he would run off.

When I finished he looked at me and asked, "Can I have it?" I reminded him he would have to quit his job with its salary and fringe benefits. I asked, "What would your wife think?" I almost insulted him.

He replied, "My wife goes with me anywhere I go."

I had no choice. The church would be his.

You should have seen him. That fellow went over to that town, and with prayer and love he began visiting the mining camps. He even went back into the mines. Then he went to the logging camps and spoke to the lumberjacks. Then he visited the poor, and whenever he found a family that had sickness or injury or trouble he would go to the stores and beg for day-old bread and other baked goods to take to them. He filled baskets with food which he distributed where there was need. Eventually he became the most loved individual in the whole country.

I went to visit and see for myself what he had done. I even helped him myself whenever I could. Within six years he had built a beautiful church and parsonage. What a day when they were dedicated! Those two beautiful new buildings stood right in a very choice spot in town. They were to me like two beautiful diamonds on green velvet. The Sunday School averaged 125, and church membership grew to 80 persons. All of this came out of the struggling little group of people with which he began.

I tell you, it is remarkable what a genuine Christian full of the Holy Ghost and faith and willing to do good works can accomplish. It is remarkable what tremendous returns can come from a fellow who is radiant with vital religion, able to display discrimination in values, and possessing a clear vision.

Give Me Something to Do

Years ago I pastored in Walla Walla, Wash. A lady in the church there who had been converted only a short time approached me with, "Give me something to do." Then she added, "But first let me tell you what I can't do. I can't play the piano. I can't sing. I can't teach, and I don't have much money to give. But I do want to do something in the church."

As I was thinking about this the Sunday School superintendent came by, so I said to him, "This lady wants something to do."

The superintendent said, "Brother Vanderpool, all the offices are filled. Just tell her to pray."

I said, "But she wants something to do." I continued, "What would you think of making her the visiting secretary for our Sunday School?"

The superintendent answered, "We don't have any office like that."

"I know, but we could make one in a minute."

"It's all right with me," agreed the superintendent.

I then turned to the lady and asked her if she would like to be the visiting secretary for our Sunday School. She responded, "I don't know. What would I have to do?"

I had to do some quick thinking, for we had just created a new position. "When Sunday School is over," I said, "you check the records. Note the absentees as well as the visitors and get the addresses for both. Then on Monday after your husband has gone to work and you have finished your housework, get in your little Ford car and call on those absentees and visitors. Find out if the absentees are sick or in trouble.

With the visitors find out if where they live makes it possible for them to become regular attenders. Then report back to me."

"I have never done anything quite like that," she said, "but I'll try."

A week later she reported. "I was visiting in a certain area and found a family that has no way to get to Sunday School. Do you suppose you could get someone to pick them up, take them to Sunday School, and then transport them home again?"

I replied, "Yes, my wife will be glad to do that. You may tell them that someone will pick them up this coming Sunday."

A few days later she reported in again that she had met another family wanting to come but having no transportation. This time I went to one of the men of the church whom I thought might offer the least resistance to the idea and asked him to care for that family. Within a few months 8 to 10 men of the congregation were regularly bringing people to Sunday School and taking them back home again.

Then at a church board meeting someone suggested we purchase a Sunday School bus just to take care of the people being contacted by our visiting secretary. There was not a single negative vote on the idea.

That lady continued her work as long as I was pastor in that church. On my last Sunday there I stood where I could see the crowd gathering. Buses unloaded their Sunday School passengers. Private cars brought in the extras. Then I saw the little lady who could not play the piano, who could not sing or teach a Sunday School class, and who did not have much money to give. But she did have a will to do something for God. Her face beamed as she watched over 100 people go into the Sunday School who would not have been there had she not responded to the urge to do something in the church.

Standing by the Salvation Army Man

My father moved his lumber mill to Brookfield, Mo. This took the family about 75 miles away from the relatives. I felt I needed to go back to where they were and preach to them.

When I arrived in my hometown I saw a Salvation Army man standing out in the street preaching to about 25 people who were watching him from the sidewalk. I stood there taking it in for a few minutes. The Salvation Army man was alone. He carried with him a big bass drum. He would beat the drum a bit and then preach until the people began to drift away. Then he would beat the drum again in order to recapture his crowd.

A little inner Voice seemed to say to me, "Go stand by that man." Then another voice seemed to suggest it would be better if I just left him alone and went on my way. Then the first Voice spoke again. "Go stand by him."

So I stepped out, walked up to where he was, and stood by him. He looked at me in surprise and then commanded me in a loud, clear voice, "Preach to the people."

It was hardly what I had expected, but I proceeded to testify and exhort for about two or three minutes before I stepped back. He picked up his drum, began beating it, and announced, "We are going to the hall." It was just a few doors away. He led the way and I followed. About 20 people followed the two of us. Once we were inside he turned to me and said, "Young man, preach to them again."

I cried and then I laughed. I told them how happy I was to be a Christian. Then I urged them to come forward and accept Christ. Two men did come and were happily converted.

The Salvation Army man shared in the joy. He gave me a big hug, saying, "God sent you to me this evening. I was nearly ready to give up, but you came and stood by me. God bless you."

IV

Stories from
My Boyhood

The Crippled Methodist Preacher

I was born and raised in Missouri. Recently I was talking to a fellow who wasn't raised in Missouri, and I told him he had a poor start in life. He went away thinking he might make it anyway.

My mother and dad fit the image of some Missourians. They were as stubborn as two government mules. Eventually they separated. They lived apart for a total of nine years. For seven of the nine years they were actually divorced.

We four boys went to live with Dad and his mother, our grandma, who came to keep house for us. Grandma was an old lady and couldn't do very much. Furthermore, everything was pretty primitive at our place.

Grandma was opposed to religion. She was dead set against it, thinking that anyone who did have any concern for it must be "loose in the upper story." As to preachers, she felt they were the biggest parasites on society you could find anywhere. This is what we were taught and the atmosphere in which we were reared.

The house we lived in was on a farm five miles out of Chillicothe, Mo. I remember a very special visitor who came to see us when I was 13 years old. He turned out to be a preacher.

My brother and I were sitting on the floor of the old farmhouse. Grandma, sitting in her chair, was smoking a pipe. It was made of clay with a cane stem stuck into it. The stem was worn pretty slick as Grandma had worked on it with her gums. You see, she didn't have any teeth.

Grandma would load her pipe and get it going good and then just sit there in a cloud of smoke. The smoke was sometimes so thick you could hardly see who she was. She had to hold onto her pipe with her hand, for if she didn't it would turn over, spilling hot embers in her lap. Then Grandma would have to get up, dust off the embers, and load up again.

On this day she was puffing away when I looked out the window and saw a man coming toward the house. I noticed that he was crippled as he limped coming down the road. He turned in at our place, opening the old, broken-down gate. He came on up and climbed the rickety steps and knocked on the door.

Grandma got up, went to the door, and opened it. There they stood facing each other. He looked at Grandma and Grandma looked at him. When he saw us boys sitting there, he asked, "May I come in?" Grandma allowed him to enter.

Once inside he saw the poverty of the place, saw the four of us on the floor, and then looked at Grandma again. He spoke. "I'm the new Methodist preacher here. I've just come to be the pastor of the Methodist church down the road here about a mile and a half away. I've been out making some calls this afternoon, and I just wondered if there would be anybody here who would be interested in coming to church. I'd like to give all of you a hearty invitation, and I'd sure be happy to have you come to our church and Sunday School."

Then he looked straight at Grandma. "And I'd really be happy to have you come."

Grandma said nothing. We said nothing.

The preacher felt his reception was anything but warm. He spoke further. "Well, I guess I ought to go. But if it's all right I'd like to have a word of prayer with you before I go." He didn't wait for Grandma to tell him it was all right to pray; he just went ahead and began to pray. Let me tell you, that old Methodist preacher reached up and took hold of the bell rope of heaven; and if you ever heard a fellow ring the bell, brother, he rang it.

Then he got on Grandma's good side. He did it by praying for the dear, gray-haired old lady who had to take care of four "obstreperous" boys. Let me tell you, after praying like that even Grandma was on his side. She had met someone who knew what a difficult time she had.

Then he prayed for all of us. Oh, how he prayed. As I sat there on the floor, only a 13-year-old lad, I said to myself, "Why, he's talking to God. I'd like to grow up to be a man who could talk to God like that. I want to learn to talk to God."

Finally he concluded with "Amen." It was the first prayer I ever remember hearing. The preacher took his hat in hand and limped out the door. As we watched him go down the steps, down the path, and past the gate, Grandma looked at us and said, "Now that is a good man." Her acknowledgment surprised me. Up until then she had always been critical of the little white church down the road.

I thought of that prayer hundreds of times before I was converted at the age of 17. When I get to heaven I plan to find that preacher. I want to thank him for his prayer and the influence it had over a 13-year-old boy's eternal future. Come to think of it, thousands have been influenced by what must have seemed like a fruitless call made by that crippled Methodist preacher.

My Ball Bat

For a while when I was a lad at home my father worked in an ax handle factory. Each day I would take his lunch to him at the noon hour. One day at the factory I talked to a young man who worked with my father. We talked about baseball. Then he inquired if I had a ball bat. When I told him I did not, he said he would make one for me. He went over to a rick of hickory wood blanks from which the ax handles were made. After looking them over he selected one with straight grain in it, brought it to me, and said, "There, that will make a good one."

I took my father's empty lunch pail and went home thinking about the ball bat the man promised to make for me. I couldn't get it out of my mind. The next day I took my father's lunch to him, expecting to see my ball bat standing up somewhere waiting for me to take it home. But when I got there, standing by the lathe was the same old stick of hickory wood. It looked no different than it did the day before, except now it was covered with dust and shavings.

The next day it was the same thing. It had not been touched. Before leaving I asked the young man if I could take the stick home and make my own ball bat out of it. He said I could.

At home I waited until Grandma had her back turned and then borrowed her best butcher knife. I took it out to the woodshed where I had the stick and began to whittle away at that tough piece of hickory wood. I soon discovered I had a pretty difficult task on my hands. I took the butcher knife back into the house and asked Grandma if I could borrow her little hatchet.

She refused. "You'll break the handle or hit it against a rock and knick it up." But I pleaded with her.

Finally she gave in and let me have the hatchet. I went back to the woodshed with it and began once again to work on that piece of hickory wood. After an hour I had made little progress. Then I remembered my father had a big double-bitted ax. Surely that would work.

I climbed up to where I could secure the big ax and then began chopping away at my stick. I couldn't hit where I

60

aimed, and soon there were big gashes in it. Looking at the scarred and chipped piece of wood, I sat down and cried. "I've ruined it. I've ruined it. That man said it would make a good ball bat, but now I've ruined it." My tears flowed freely.

Next day I decided to take my stick back to the man at the mill. First, though, I cut off the long splinters and removed the loose chips. I tried to hide it behind me so no one would see it as I carried it along with my father's lunch.

After giving the lunch pail to my father, I looked up the young man. I showed him my stick, scars and all. "I didn't do a very good job," I muttered. He smiled and said, "Here, let me have it."

He put down his own lunch, took the stick, walked over to the lathe, and fastened it in place. Turning on the power caused it to whirl around. He then picked up a wood chisel and began to work on it. Chips and shavings flew everywhere. I thought, perhaps he can make something of it after all. He never stopped till he went deep, even deeper than the deepest scar I had made. Then he stopped the motor and lifted it from the lathe. It was a beautiful ball bat.

Next he took it over to the sander and smoothed it up. Then he put it on a brush and waxing machine. Finally he handed it to me. "There," he said, "is the ball bat I promised you."

I laughed and headed for home, waving my ball bat—a very happy boy.

Life sometimes is like that. After we have almost ruined it through impatience and through ignorance we only need to bring it back to Jesus. We give it to Him, splinters and all, acknowledging we have failed. He in return gives to us a life made new, shaped and fashioned according to His plan and will for us.

61

The Star Mittens

One morning my grandmother promised me a pair of "star" mittens. Her promise thrilled my boyish heart. How very much I wanted new mittens with a star on the back of them.

I asked her in the afternoon if they were ready. She said they were not. That night I asked again. "No," she said, "I don't have them yet."

Next morning I got up early and asked again. She scolded me and said, "Don't bother me now, for I still don't have them."

At other times I went to her during the day. The answer was always the same. "They are not ready."

Then she spoke to my father and asked him to go to town and get some yarn. She told him she had promised me some star mittens, and I was giving her no rest until they were knitted.

The next morning I dared ask once again. "Here," she said, "are your star mittens. I sat up half the night knitting them for you."

If people would be half as interested in the promise of our Heavenly Father as I was in my grandmother's promise, they could be filled with the Holy Spirit before the day closed.

Go to It, Cotton!

Years ago when I was just a small fellow we lived in Chillicothe, Mo. One day they were having a tournament race in nearby Kirksville. In our school was a boy whose name was Cotton. We called him that because his hair was almost white.

His real name was Adams, but he was such a blond we nick-named him Cotton.

He could run. He could run fast and far, and we thought if we could just get him over to Kirksville he could win the prize in the tournament there. We got together in our school and collected the necessary $4.00 to send him.

Then we thought we should send someone with him so that he wouldn't be over there alone. We selected a fellow named Jones to accompany him. We called him Jonesie. We chose him because he was a one-man cheering section. You can't imagine how much noise old Jonesie could make when he really wanted to do so. We took up another collection and purchased a ticket so that Jonesie could go to Kirksville with Cotton. Cotton would run and Jonesie would cheer for him.

When they arrived Cotton was signed up for the race. Jonesie was assigned to a certain area in the stands where space had been reserved for 40 to 50 fans from Chillicothe. But, of course, Jonesie was all we had. He was the only cheerer for Cotton. But at least there was one.

The pistol was fired and the racers were off. They had to make it several times around the track. When they passed the Chillicothe fan area Jonesie would stand up and yell as loud as he could, "Go to it, Cotton!" Cotton responded by putting on a burst of speed.

He was doing quite well in the race when he passed Jonesie for the last lap. As Cotton headed for the finish line, Jonesie stood up with his red sweater in his hand. He took the sweater by the sleeve, swung it around and around over his head, and yelled for all he was worth, "Go to it, Cotton!" Cotton leaped ahead and won the race.

When they returned to Chillicothe we met them both. We carried Cotton around on our shoulders and whooped it up because he had won the race. After we had carried on for quite a while we put him down.

Cotton said he had something to report about the race himself. "Listen, fellows. When I came around the track for the last time heading for the finish line, I looked over in the stands and saw Jonesie. There he was, waving that red sweater and yelling for all he was worth. That did it. I gave those last few yards everything I had and won the race. But I never could have done it without Jonesie."

Well, Jonesie not only could yell but he was also very large. In fact, he was too big for us to carry him around on our shoulders. But we let him know how glad we were he had been there to cheer for Cotton.

In this race which Christians are running it may be you aren't in the foreground. You may not be in the field where all can see you. In fact, you may be off to the side. But you are still important to the race. If you aren't a runner, be a cheerer. Shout the runner on. Give him everything you've got. Make him aware of your support. When he wins you win, too, and all share in the victory.

What Christ Did for Our Family

After two years of separation my mother and father were divorced. My brothers and I lived with my father and grandmother. Mother went to live near her folks. Six years after the divorce and eight years after the separation my mother was converted. She had come under the influence of a Free Methodist church, and there she came to Christ. Then she moved to our county seat, a town located only five miles from where we were living.

I heard about her being so close by. I also received word she was doing laundry at her home to make a living. It had been several years since I had seen her, so I began to visit her.

She, of course, inquired about all, including Dad as well as the boys and Grandma. She seemed to harbor no ill feelings.

One day she asked me if I didn't want to give my heart to God. I told her, "No! I need that myself. I couldn't live without it." Such were the depths of my ignorance on spiritual matters.

I began visiting Mother each Saturday evening. None of the rest of the family knew that I was doing so. They simply thought I was out having a good time.

I shared what little spending money I had with my mother. She made 25 to 40 cents for doing a big wash. My 20 cents helped a little. She was always so grateful for what I did.

For a period of three weeks I didn't get in to see her. I received a phone call telling me that my mother was very ill. My father knew I had received a call and inquired about it. As I started to leave he asked where I was going. I replied I was just going for a ride. When he pressed further I finally told him I was going to see Mother. I thought he would be angry and tell me not to go. To my surprise, however, he asked to go with me.

He stayed in the buggy while I went in. Mother had a burning fever and her left arm was swollen double its normal size. She asked if I had come alone. I told her Dad was with me. She asked for him to come in.

They greeted one another and Dad held her hand in his. He left for a while and returned, announcing he had made arrangements for Mother to be placed in the hospital. When she finally recuperated Dad purchased a washing machine and gave it to her so she wouldn't have to wash by hand.

A year later Dad approached me at his lumber mill and said, "Son, I am thinking of getting married. What would you think of that?"

I was dumbfounded and finally said, "It would all depend on who you marry."

He said, "I am thinking about marrying that woman you go to see each Saturday night."

I replied, "You mean Mother? Why, Dad, that would be the smartest move you ever made in your life."

Nine years after the separation and seven years after the divorce Mother and Dad were married to each other again. The mill was moved to a new location and a house secured nearby for the family. We were all together again including, of course, Grandma.

Mother insisted now on family prayers, morning and night. Dad, although not a Christian himself, insisted on everyone cooperating. All but Grandma were expected to kneel for these prayers. Mother did the praying. She prayed for all of us, and I began to feel the impact of her intercession. I felt she was praying too long, so I decided to leave home.

In the meantime my brother Marion got saved down at the Free Methodist church. I was curious to see what he looked like now that he had got religion. He came to where I was working. When he arrived I was playing cards with a group of friends. We asked him to join us, but he refused, saying that he had quit such activity. He sat, smoking his pipe, while we played cards. I thought to myself that it was funny his religion hadn't made him quit smoking his pipe. I used that to reason that I didn't want his kind of religion. Later Marion did feel smoking was wrong and gave it up.

I had a Sunday off from where I worked and decided to go home for the day. When I got there the house was empty. All were in church. They returned about one o'clock, and we had Sunday dinner together. Late in the afternoon I started to leave. My mother asked if I couldn't stay and go to church with them that night. I lied by telling her I had chores to do. It was my day off, but I simply didn't want to get pulled into going to church with them. Mother seemed very disappointed.

As I was leaving I felt bad about lying and decided if it meant so much to them I'd just as well stay and go with them. I told them I decided I'd let one of the other fellows go ahead and do the chores. Of course, I had not really told the truth at any time.

On the way I took over the conversation, for all seemed so gloomy. I told jokes, poked fun, and laughed loud and long. Then I got sore because I didn't think they were responding.

At church I continued to be miserable. The people sang and prayed. Then there were testimonies. My brother Marion stood up and talked, telling how happy he was now that he was a Christian. The district elder of the Free Methodist Conference preached. His subject was sin. He said it was a sin to steal, to lie, to fight, to drink, to desecrate the Sabbath, and to hold hard feelings against people. I was guilty on all counts.

Then he began to talk about Jesus and His love. He spoke about Christ's sacrifice and His forgiveness. He said the invitation was for all. But then he proceeded to picture a burning hell that awaits everyone who rejects the call to pardon. I could wait no longer. I stepped out and made my way to the mourner's bench.

Now I had heard them talk of a mourner's bench. I figured it was a thing you would go and lie on while people gathered around and mourned over you. I was prepared for anything and willing to do anything. But when I went forward an elderly lady said, "Son, kneel right here."

That night at the first altar call I ever heard I sought Christ as my Savior. I sought Him with a broken heart, and in true repentance I promised to change my way of living, to return things I had stolen, and to ask forgiveness of those I had wronged. I promised to bear the cross of Christ and to be a witness for Him.

They began to sing a chorus and my faith touched Him. I was converted, born again if you please.

About that time I heard the cry of a brokenhearted man. It was my dad. In a few minutes he too was gloriously converted. Mother, Dad, Marion, and I took over the place, marching about, shouting and celebrating. We laughed and cried and testified all the way home that night. It was March 27, 1909. I was 17 years old.

The Early Morning Ride

One day I was in a little town when I happened to see two young men I knew. They were Carl and Harry, two boys with whom I had experienced a lot of trouble when we had been in school together. I walked by them, not sure they had noticed me. The Lord spoke to me and told me I should fix things up with them. I prayed about it and promised God I would do so. Then God seemed to say, "When?" I said I would do it the next morning.

Early the following day I arose and prayed further about the matter. I then saddled my horse and rode out five miles to where they lived. Their mother greeted me at the door. I told her who I was and that I wanted to see Carl and Harry. Because she could see that I had been crying, she decided I would be harmless, so she called her boys.

Harry came out of the bedroom. I stuck my hand out to him and explained to him I was trying to be a Christian. I then told him how badly I felt about our trouble and that I was asking for his forgiveness. He took me by the hand and said, "It's OK, Vandy. I was as much to blame as you were."

Then Carl came out into the room where we were talking. I said about the same thing to him. He looked straight at me and said, "It's OK, Van. Let's forget the whole thing."

We shook hands as I told them I wanted to be a real Christian. With that the mother put her hand on my head and said, "I believe you are one already. May God bless you."

I was glad I had cleared things up as we were all friends from then on.

Old Bill and My Blowup

Although a new Christian, I was trying to be a good one. One hot day I was cultivating corn with Old Bill, our mule. The corn was about waist high, and Old Bill would just stop wherever he wanted to, reach down, and bite the top out of a stalk of corn. I would jerk on the reins and yell at him to keep going.

That night after returning to the barn, I was taking off the mule's harness when he raised his foot, stomping at the flies, and proceeded to bring his foot down on mine. It felt like he had broken all my toes. Like a flash I swore at Old Bill. I hit him over the head with a bridle and struck him several times across the ribs.

Then I realized what I had done. I felt terrible that I had taken God's name in vain and felt just as badly that I had hit Old Bill across the head with those heavy bridle bits. I knew I had sinned. I had sinned against God by what I had said and done.

I went to my room without eating. On my knees I begged God to forgive me. I felt sorry for poor Old Bill. He certainly didn't know any better. I felt badly about how unchristian I had been.

About 12 o'clock I arose, dressed, and went back to the barn. When I opened the door Old Bill began to nicker. He was glad I had come. I gave him two ears of corn (not just the usual one) and put my arms around his neck. I even asked him to forgive me for hitting him with the heavy bridle bit. Then I asked God again to forgive me for swearing at Old Bill.

I believed Christ saw my sorrow and forgave the whole matter. I was able to finally go to bed with a clear conscience.

My Struggle with Tobacco

At the time of my conversion at age 17 I could look back on nearly a lifetime of using tobacco. I had begun when I was just a little fellow. I would even go to school with chewing tobacco in my mouth. Once in the schoolroom, when the teacher wasn't looking I would spit into the chalk box. I really didn't think too much about it.

Even after I was converted I smoked my pipe and chewed tobacco. All the while I was happy in the Lord. I knew God had forgiven me, and it never dawned on me that this might be a hindrance to my relationship with God or that it might be something wrong to do.

One day as I was driving my team of horses down the road on the way to the field I was praying and worshiping the Lord. I said, "Dear Lord, Thou hast been so good to me. Now what can I do for Thee?"

I seemed to hear a Voice speaking: "If you want to be a good example and show people what My grace can do, you could give up your tobacco, and then people would see how you have really changed. They would see how different you are and that you are really going to live for Me."

"Well," I said, "all right. That's what I'll do. I'll give it up."

At the time I was smoking my pipe. I came to a culvert where a stream of water was running through. As I drove over the culvert I took my pipe and tossed it into the water. Now, I've always said it was the devil who made that pipe hang up in the forks of a little willow sprout which reached out over the stream about two or three feet. Each day I'd see that pipe hanging in the willow sprout whenever I drove over the culvert.

One day I had just finished dinner when I had a strong craving to smoke. My, how I wanted to smoke! I thought, Say, I remember where that pipe is.

I went down to the culvert, waded out into the water, retrieved my pipe, and loaded it up. I struck a match to it and went off down the road in a cloud of smoke. It was just great!

But I hadn't gone far when I heard the little Voice again. "I thought you said you were going to give that up for Me." I realized I had broken a promise. I knew I had sinned against God in that I hadn't been obedient in what I had promised to do. I drove off the road into the field and stopped the team. I got out and dug a hole in the ground. I then put my pipe into the hole and covered it up with a nice mound of dirt over it. Although it really didn't deserve it, I gave my pipe a decent burial. I then knelt down on both knees right on the grave. I prayed, "Lord, by Thy grace I'll die before I'll ever touch that stuff again." I meant it. I've never touched it since.

One of the big problems people have is that when they throw things like that away, they watch where they go. I might have been all right if I hadn't seen where that pipe went. But God wants us to lay aside anything that may make us stumble or stagger or that may be a hindrance to someone else. Lay it aside and claim victory in Jesus' name.

Sanctified

A few days after my conversion I felt I should try to get other folks converted as well. I witnessed to friends and neighbors, telling them of the peace I had found. At the same time I also began to feel the need of something more in my religion. My quick temper caused me to say or do things I knew displeased God. Swearing and cursing the horses or other animals on the farm was a habit I had carried over from the time I was a little fellow. I knew I would have to get victory over all of this.

Through reading the Bible, praying, hearing people testify, along with my continued battle with a sharp temper, I was soon convinced I needed to be sanctified. I somehow felt that receiving this experience must be my objective at the next prayer meeting to be held. Although the little Free Methodist church we were now attending was in charge, the prayer meeting was held in a private home.

All day before the meeting I was confident in my heart I would come through. My fear was that perhaps the pastor wouldn't like it, for someone had told me he didn't believe in sanctification. Obviously I was misinformed, for the pastor spoke on the subject of sanctification in the prayer service. He concluded his message by placing five chairs in front of the room and inviting those who wanted to be sanctified and were ready to make a lifelong commitment to God to kneel at the chairs. I stepped out and knelt at the middle chair.

A 45-year-old brother from Kansas who happened to be visiting in our community knelt by my side. Three others came and knelt at the other chairs. We all prayed.

After I had said yes to God on every proposition presented to me, I put up both hands in total surrender. Someone said, "Believe, young man."

I said, "I do believe."

The question went further. "What do you believe?"

I said, "I believe I'll be lost if I don't get sanctified." I was then admonished to trust Christ to keep His Word.

I thought for a moment and said, "I do trust Him." My burden was lifted. The Holy Spirit took possession and sanctified me that night. That was a great night—May 20, 1909—just over two months after my conversion.

The brother from Kansas next to me also prayed through. I can hear him yet as he declared, "Oh, that 20 years ago I could have had this experience. I would have been spared such an up and down life."

Many years later I saw him again in Kansas. We rejoiced together because of a wonderful experience we had received in that prayer meeting back in Missouri.

Uncle Hy

My Uncle Hy, a circuit court judge, lived in the northern part of Missouri. I was still a new Christian and had been sanctified for about three months when I went over to his part of the state to visit him. I hadn't seen him for three or four years.

It was nine o'clock in the morning when I knocked on the door. He opened the door and took one look at me. Then he began to laugh. I soon discovered he was making fun at me.

"Ha, ha ha," he laughed, "they tell me you got religion."

I said, "Yes, Uncle Hy, I've been saved."

He laughed again. "Ha, ha. So you got to heaven, did you?"

I said, "No, Uncle Hy, I didn't get to heaven, but I sure did get awfully close."

Then he began to ridicule the Bible. All day long he continued making fun of my religion. He tore away at the very foundations of my faith. But about every 15 or 20 minutes I seemed to hear a little Voice telling me that everything was going to be all right.

Late that evening Uncle Hy looked at me and grinned before he spoke. "Well, Ike, I suppose you'd like to pray before you go to bed." It was further ridicule on his part, and I knew it. But something seemed to prompt me to say that I would indeed like to pray.

I knelt on the old rag carpet. As I turned to kneel I felt five pairs of eyes watching every move. There was Grandma, two of my cousins, Aunt Jane, and Uncle Hy. I had no more than hit the rag carpet when my wires were connected. I began to pray.

God blessed my soul, and I prayed some more. I stomped the floor and pounded the chair where I was kneeling. I shouted and cried. I had a real celebration as I prayed. What a wonderful time I had! When I finally got back to my feet I looked over and there was poor old Grandma. She had slid off her chair and was on her knees. Aunt Jane was on her knees as well. The cousins looked stunned. And Uncle Hy was just sitting there with his hands up over his face. Tears were running down between his fingers and dripping on the carpet.

He looked at me and said, "Ike, what is it that makes you shout so much?"

I said, "Uncle Hy, if you knew that all your sins were gone and that you could stand before God without one thing between you and Him, as innocent as a child, don't you think you would shout too?"

He looked at me and quietly said, "Yes, Ike, I believe I would."

V

Stories
That Teach

Hog Ears

In my early ministry I received an invitation to conduct a revival meeting in a schoolhouse located in the sand hills of eastern Colorado. Arrangements were made for me to stay in the home of one of the local homesteaders. Everything was quite primitive. Sleeping quarters were in a shedlike room attached to the house. The beds were coil springs with corn shuck bedticks placed on them.

Our meals were eaten in the kitchen. The husband and father sat at the head of the table. Next to him on his right sat his wife. On around the table were his three boys, ages 14, 12, and 10. On around the table and to the left of my host was the spot reserved for me.

At the table I would be asked to offer thanks before the serving ritual began. First the old man would rake from the serving bowl a generous portion for himself. He then passed it to his wife. From there it went to his three hungry boys. Finally, I was given what was left. This procedure was followed each mealtime for a week. Obviously the man had little regard for me as a preacher and let his feelings be known.

One day he butchered a hog. He didn't get a good scald on it which left a lot of hair on the hog's head. But the pork which was served for meals the next day or two was appreciated.

The man did attend the meetings in the schoolhouse. I preached against sin, selfishness, and dishonesty. I preached that God required people to be born again, that they must be filled with the Spirit and walk in the light.

We had a few seekers in the meeting, but my host was not one of them. In fact, he would hardly speak to me. I had made some good friends in the community including the three boys with whom I stayed.

When I was about to leave, the oldest boy offered to take me back to my own homestead in their spring wagon. Before leaving, I said to my host, "Would you sell me about a dollar's worth of that pork?"

He exploded, "There you go, begging for food while this has been the poorest revival meeting we have ever had here. It's disgusting. In fact, all of us are disgusted with you."

I was startled and began to apologize. "Well, sir, I just thought my little wife back at the homestead would appreciate a change from jackrabbit and pumpkin. But that's okay, Brother."

I turned to get into the wagon. It was not my desire to leave with him thinking I was in a huff myself, so I endeavored to show a good spirit in the matter. He went into the house and quickly returned. He was carrying a paper sack. He set it beside me and said, "Here's your meat."

I reached into my pocket for a silver dollar and offered it to him. He said, "Keep your money. You begged for it, now you have it. So get along."

When we arrived at my house I took out the silver dollar once again and gave it to the oldest boy who had brought me. "You and your brothers take this and get something you would like with it."

He refused, saying, "No, Daddy would whip me until I couldn't walk if I did." I didn't insist but wished him God's blessings as he drove off.

Entering the house, I found my wife was preparing dinner. After we had greeted one another she asked what I had in the paper sack. I told her it was some pork which had been given me by my host at the revival meeting. I knew she would be glad to get it.

She took the sack and we both noticed it rattled a bit as it exchanged hands. She looked in and then asked, "Did you see what was in this sack?"

I replied that I hadn't looked in.

"Come here and see," she said.

I looked in, and there were two hairy, dirty hog ears along with a piece of hairy jowl taken from the hog's cheek. Nothing more. We both cried a bit. But then I got tickled and began to laugh. "I knew the old man was stirred," I said, "but I didn't know he was stirred that much."

From that time on I never thought of that man by his rightful name. I just thought of him as Brother Hog Ears.

Several years later I was campground manager about 20 miles from where Brother Hog Ears lived. The day before our camp was to open I looked up and saw a team of mules pulling a covered wagon coming our way. As it came closer I said, "Why, if it isn't old Brother Hog Ears."

As he drove up I asked if he was coming to the camp meeting. He said he planned to stay for the entire period.

I thought to myself that this would be an excellent opportunity to return good for evil. I said to him, "Good. Drive right in here. This is a fine spot close to everything. Leave your wagon, put the harness underneath, and take your team just down the road where there is a fenced pasture with plenty of grass and water. You'll have no worry for 10 days. If there is anything I can do for you, just let me know.

Our district superintendent was Dr. A. E. Sanner, and C. W. Ruth was camp evangelist. In response to Brother Ruth's preaching old Brother Hog Ears went to the altar. It was about the third night of the camp. I didn't go near him.

The next day I heard groans coming from inside his covered wagon. I told my wife that I thought he would have to say something or other about those hog's ears before he would get through to victory.

The next afternoon while standing by the big camp tent I heard prayers and groans again coming from inside the covered wagon. Shortly, the flaps of the wagon were thrown back, and out came old Brother Hog Ears. He walked down the tongue of the wagon onto the ground over to where I was standing talking to some men.

When he was just a few feet away he suddenly fell to his knees and began crawling toward me. He would have put his arms around my legs but I stepped back. He looked up at me with tears streaming down his cheeks. "Oh, Brother Vanderpool," he said, "can you ever forgive me for putting those dirty, hairy hog ears in that sack and sending them home to your hungry wife?"

I said, "Oh, yes," and I put an arm around him to help him to his feet. We hugged each other and promised each other we would meet someday in a better country by the grace of God.

When he returned to his home he was a changed man. He prayed, testified, apologized to neighbors, convincing all that he was indeed different than he had been.

When he died it was discovered that he had not only adequately provided for his family but for his church as well. From his estate, money was designated for the purpose of building a camp meeting tabernacle for the Colorado District.

I never speak the name Hog Ears without feeling a genuine love for a man changed by the grace of God.

The Fur-lined Gloves

Years ago when our family was homesteading in eastern Colorado, I gave my brother Marion a fine pair of fur-lined gloves for Christmas. They really were very nice. I thought they would be great for driving his team of horses into town or to church. In fact, the family felt I had given him a very special gift.

The next spring I went to the farm to see how everyone was getting along. My brother Marion was not in the house. His wife told me he had gone to the back side of the place to check on a broken fence. I rode out to where he was working on some old barbed wire. As I got closer I was surprised to see he had on the beautiful fur-lined gloves I had given him. They were dirty and scratched, with holes punched in them. Bits of fur were showing through the holes. They were ruined for Sunday wear.

I was upset about it and was just about ready to say something to him when I thought, But whose gloves are they? I had given them to him. Now they were his. If he wanted to use them in such a way, that was up to him. I didn't say anything. But I did learn a leasson from it.

When we give ourselves in consecration to God, we become His property. If He has some barbed wire which needs mending out on the back side of the Kingdom and He wants me to do it, then that is His business. He can use me in any assignment He wants. I must simply honor Him in faithful service wherever He chooses. The appointed task may be rough or it may be smooth. It may be hard or it may be easy. It makes no difference, for I am His property.

Man in Chains

Some years ago I was driving through a little town in southern New Mexico. A group of people had gathered on the street corner. One man out in the street was talking to the crowd on the sidewalk. He was calling for people to gather around him.

Being of a curious nature, I parked my car and walked back to see what this was all about. I thought the fellow in the street might be preaching and that he perhaps needed someone to say "Amen" for him.

It wasn't that at all. In front of him this fellow had laid down 13 pieces of chain. On the end of each chain was an open padlock. He was asking for two strong men to come out of the crowd and bind him with those 13 chains. Two big, husky men volunteered. They acted like they enjoyed it. They put a chain around his wrists, behind his back, and then pulled it as tight as possible before snapping the padlock shut. They repeated the process with another chain around the man's waist. They eventually used all the chains, grinning as they did so, seemingly having the time of their lives. It was a field day for them.

I stood there and watched the fellow. He was now all bent over. His eyes appeared to be bulging from their sockets. The veins stood out on his forehead. I said to myself, "That poor, crazy fellow. They're going to kill him."

Then I began to think how the devil puts chains on people. He puts them on young men and young women as well as older folk. He pulls them as tight as he can, snapping the padlocks shut; all the while full of grins and delights as he yanks, binding them with habits and appetites and associations, cutting grooves in their nature, making them slaves to sin. I stood there and cried. Tears ran down my face as I thought how the devil is binding people all over the country.

I thought of our young people who are playing with sin, seemingly unconcerned over the consequences. When you play with sin it will enslave and enchain you. I got all broken up standing there thinking about how people are bound by sin. But when those two men finished putting the chains on that fellow, he said, "All of you take out your watches. I'll be a free man in 30 seconds."

What happened then I have never been able to figure out. He said, "Go," and all at once he just seemed to shrivel up. He got those chains up over his wrists, down off his shoulders, over his hips, past his knees and ankles, and over his feet. In just 28 seconds that man stepped out of the pile of chains at his feet a free man.

Then I got blessed. I said to myself, I see it. I see it. That's the picture! Those men and women who have been bound for years with habits that have cut grooves in their nature until it looks as though they will never be released from them, can be free. We have a Savior who is able to save to the uttermost all those who come to God by Him. That man or woman, that young person, however tightly they may be bound, can have those chains broken and be set free.

I thank God for this possibility.

Jesus Is Our Pattern

I went to help in the building of a home mission church. The head carpenter assigned me the task of sawing some studding. He said to me, "Here are the two-by-fours, and here's the pattern you are to follow. Cut about 50 of these."

I started right in. I took a two-by-four and laid it across two sawhorses. I then took the pattern and laid it on the two-by-four. After marking the wood I let the pattern drop. Then I sawed the studding in two and let it drop. I continued in this manner until I had about 30 studding cut and stacked.

Then I noticed that all the studding didn't look to be the same length. I measured them and found each one to be a trifle longer than the one next to it. This went on clear through the pile of studding until I found there was an inch and a half difference between the first and the last.

Then I saw what I had done. I had used the pattern given me only once. Then I had used the last one I had sawed as a pattern for the next. Fortunately, all of the studding were just a little too long. In order to save the lumber all I had to do was saw all of them again, but this time carefully using the pattern which had been given me.

The lesson learned that day was clear. For life to be meaningful and useful, the pattern given us by Jesus himself must be carefully followed.

Stopped at the Line

Years ago I received an invitation to go over into Canada to hold a camp meeting. We were living in the state of Washington at the time. I asked my wife if she thought we should accept the invitation, and she felt we should. So we went.

We got into our Pontiac into which we had packed our things, and headed for Canada. Our route took us through Spokane and Priest River and finally the border town of Kingsgate. I noticed that flags were waving in the breeze, and men in uniform were to be seen about the place. I thought little of it and just drove right across the border into the country of Canada.

We hadn't gone very far when I heard a shrill whistle which obviously was a warning to stop the car. A uniformed man approached us and said, "And, if I may ask, just where are you going?"

I replied that we were going to Canada. "For what purpose?" he inquired further.

"Oh, I'm going to hold a camp meeting," I said.

"A camp meeting? What is that?"

"Well, it is where people come in from all over the country. A large tent is pitched and we have services in it three or four times a day."

"I take it from this that you are a minister. Is that correct?" asked the uniformed man further.

"Yes, sir, I'm a preacher," was my response.

Then he asked, "Are you an elder?"

84

"Yes, sir," I replied.

"May I see your elder's orders?" he now asked.

My elder's orders were hanging on my study wall back in Walla Walla, so I had to say, "No, sir, I don't have them with me."

He persisted, "Do you have anything to prove you are an elder?" I happened to remember that I had the printed minutes of the last district assembly with me. I knew that on page 5 of those minutes was a list of all the elders on our district and that my name would be there. I didn't know in which of the 11 suitcases we had with us the minutes would be found, but I began to search. Eventually I did find the minutes and turned to page 5. I pointed down the page to my name, "Vanderpool," and said, "There it is. That's my name, Vanderpool."

Looking at me intently, he asked, "Sir, now do you have anything on you to prove that you are D. I. Vanderpool?" I took out my billford and showed him my driver's license. He said, "Well now, I see you are D. I. Vanderpool, that you are an elder in your church, and that you are going to hold a camp meeting in my country. I hope you have a wonderful time, and we'll be seeing you again when you come back through."

I jammed those suitcases back into the trunk, got into the car, and started again down the road. You know, I had been stopped at the line. I had been embarrassed.

I'm coming to another line one of these days. It's not the line between the United States and Canada. It is the line which divides this world from a better one. And when I get there I don't want to be stopped and embarrassed. I thank God I won't have to be.

God's Ambassador from heaven, the Holy Spirit, is here in this world to sign the documents, fix a seal to them so that I can have my naturalization papers ready when I come to that line. Then I can go sweeping across right through the gates, washed in the blood of the Lamb. I won't have to worry or wait or be stopped. I'll not be embarrassed at the line.

Sin Is like Fire

While driving in the state of Idaho, I came down over a hill and saw a truck loaded with hay. It had gone off the road and caught on fire. Some men were there trying to put the fire out but couldn't get close enough to do so because it was so hot. They had shovels which they were using to throw dirt on the fire. But because of the intense heat they couldn't get close enough to do any good.

Three days later I came back on the same road and there, off to the side, was the burned-out frame of what had once been a beautiful truck. The fire had completely destroyed it, leaving nothing but warped and twisted metal. It gave me a new appreciation for what fire can do.

Sin is like a fire. It may start from a mere spark but if left unchecked will destroy everything in its path. It will leave lives that are warped and twisted, nothing but piles of junk, damned by the fires of sin.

The Manager Is Watching

A caretaker in a railroad depot built a reputation for being the best in the whole division. He dutifully cleaned, dusted, ventilated, and regularly checked the temperature. He was courteous to passengers, visitors, and his fellow laborers. He was always on time.

Someone talked to him about his general attitude toward the railroad company. He was asked about his duties, his colleagues, and how long he had worked at the job. Inquiry was

86

made as to how he could stand the complaints of so many and yet be courteous to everybody.

He had an answer. "See that big window over at the other end of the depot? That is the window of the general manager of this whole operation. He can see every move I make. He holds my job in his hands, and I want to please him."

Jesus is my Manager. He sees every move I make. He hears everything I say. He knows all the thoughts of my mind. I want to please Him.

Making an Altar Call

One Sunday when I was serving as pastor I did two important things in one service. First, I received new members into the fellowship of the church. Then before the service was concluded I gave an altar call for sinners to come forward and get saved.

There was a businessman present who was attending our church for the first time. He sat through the entire service including the altar call when I begged and pleaded for people to come forward. Afterwards I greeted him, and he said, "You know, I got the surprise of my life tonight. I thought the Church of the Nazarene had standards."

I asked why he should now think that we didn't have any. "You got up and begged for people to come and join your church tonight. Now suppose some old drunk or bum or someone all messed up in their life had come down there and joined your church."

"Oh," I replied, "my brother, you didn't understand. I wasn't pleading for people to come down and join the church. I was urging them to get saved, get religion, get straightened out so that later on they could join the church. Then they would be eligible to do so."

When I think about it there is something special about the mourner's bench. It's a great arrangement, for here is a fellow all tied up, messed up with all kinds of sins. Then we get him to the altar and there bring him in contact with Jesus Christ. His life is revolutionized. His hopes and desires are changed about. He becomes a new man.

We need to have holy faith which we believe will bring Christ and the seeker into contact with one another, and victory will be experienced.

The Warning Red Light

Heavy rains had flooded the rivers in California. A bridge across a swift torrent had washed out. As night fell a patrolman had been stationed there to stop oncoming cars.

The patrolman saw a fast car approaching. He stepped out into the center of the road, waving his red light. The driver did not slacken his speed. Instead, he drove even faster. The patrolman knew that 200 yards further the bridge was out. The car would plunge into a raging stream and all would be lost.

He swung the red light wildly. He cried out as the car went by. Then he saw the car go out of sight. The lights vanished and all was black as midnight.

The patrolman hurried to the river. The car was not to be seen. Only the roar of the torrent could be heard. When the flood receded the car was found. Its occupants were not. No one ever knew who was driving the car that passed the swinging red light.

God is watching. He swings a red light of warning. He has been trying to stop men and women before they come to a tragic end. The storm is on, but God is faithful. Give heed to Him and be saved.